The Flowers of Evil

Charles Baudelaire

Charles Baudelaire

THREE DRAFTS OF A PREFACE

I

PREFACE

France is passing through a period of vulgarity. Paris, a center radiating universal stupidity. Despite Molière and Béranger, no one would ever have believed that France would take to the road of progress at such a rate. matters of art, terrae incognitae.
Great Men are stupid.

My book may have done some good; I do not regret that. It may have done harm; I do not rejoice at that.

The aim of poetry. This book is not made for my wives, my daughters, or my sisters.

Every sin, every crime I have related has been imputed to me.

Hatred and contempt as forms of amusement. Elegists are vulgar scum. Et verbum caro factum est. The poet is of no party. Otherwise, he would be a mere mortal.

The Devil. Original sin. Man as good. If you would, you could be the Tyrant's favorite; it is more difficult to love God than to believe in Him. On the other hand, it is more difficult for people nowadays to believe in the Devil than to love him. Everyone smells him and no one believes in him. Sublime sublety of the Devil.

A soul to my liking. The scene. --Thus, novelty. --The Epigraph. --D'Aurevilly. --The Renaissance. --Gérard de Nerval. --We are all hanged or hangable.

I have included a certain amount of filth to please the gentleman of the press. They have proved ungrateful.

II

PREFACE TO THE FLOWERS

It is not for my wives, my daughters, or my sisters that this book has been written; nor for the wives, daughters, or sisters of my neighbors. I leave that to those who have some reason to confuse good deeds with fine language.

I know the passionate lover of fine style exposes himself to the hatred of the masses; but no respect for humanity, no false modesty, no conspiracy, no universal suffrage will ever force me to speak the unspeakable jargon of this age, or to confuse ink with virtue.

Certain illustrious poets have long since divided among themselves the more flowery provinces of the realm of poetry. I have found it amusing, and the more pleasant because the task was more difficult, to extract beauty from Evil. This book, which is quintessentially useless and absolutely innocent, was written with no other aim than to divert myself and to practice my passionate taste for the difficult.

Some have told me that these poems might do harm; I have not rejoiced at that. Others, good souls, that they might do good; and that has given me no regret. I was equally surprised at the former's fear and the latter's hope, which only served to prove once again that this age has unlearned all the classical notions of literature.

Despite the encouragement a few celebrated pedants have given to man's natural stupidity, I should never have believed our country could move with such speed along the road of progress. The world has taken on a thickness of vulgarity that raises a spiritual man's contempt to the violence of a passion. But there are those happy hides so thick that poison itself could not penetrate them.

I had intended, at first, to answer numerous criticisms and at the same time to explain a few quite simple questions that have been totally obscured by modern enlightenment: What is poetry? What is its aim? On the distinction between the Good and the Beautiful; on the Beauty of Evil; that rhythm

and rhyme answer the immortal need in man for monotony, symmetry, and surprise; on adapting style to subject; on the vanity and danger of inspiration, etc., etc.; but this morning I was so rash as to read some of the public newspapers; suddenly an indolence of the weight of twenty atmospheres fell upon me, and I was stopped, faced by the appalling uselessness of explaining anything whatever to anyone whatever. Those who know can divine me, and for those who can not or will not understand, it would be fruitless to pile up explanations.
C.B.

How the artist, by a prescribed series of exercises, can proportionately increase his originality;

How poetry is related to music through prosody, whose roots go deeper into the human soul than any classical theory indicates;

That French poetry possesses a mysterious and unrecognized prosody, like the Latin and English languages;

Why any poet who does not know exactly how many rhymes each word has is incapable of expressing any idea whatever;

That the poetic phrase can imitate (and in this, it is like the art of music and the science of mathematics) a horizontal line, an ascending or descending vertical line; that it can rise straight up to heaven without losing its breath, or go perpendicularly to hell with the velocity of any weight; that it can follow a spiral, describe a parabola, or zigzag, making a series of superimposed angles;

That poetry is like the arts of painting, cooking, and cosmetics in its ability to express every sensation of sweetness or bitterness, beatitude or horror, by coupling a certain noun with a certain adjective, in analogy or contrast;

How, by relying on my principle and using the knowledge which I guarantee to teach him in twenty lessons, any man can learn to compose a tragedy that will be no more hooted at than another, or line up a poem long enough to be as dull as any epic known.

A difficult matter, to rise to that divine callousness! For, despite my most commendable efforts, even I have not been able to resist the desire to please my contemporaries, as witness in several places, laid on like make-up, certain patches of base flattery aimed at democracy, and even a certain amount of filth meant to excuse the dreariness of my subject. But the gentlemen of the press have proved ungrateful for tender attentions of this kind, I have eliminated every trace of both, so far as possible, from this new edition.

I propose, in order to prove again the excellence of my method, to apply it in the near future to celebrating the pleasures of devotion and the raptures of military glory, though I have never known either.

Notes on plagiarisms. --Thomas Gray. Edgar Poe (2 passages). Longfellow (2 passages). Statius. Virgil (the whole of Andromache). Aeschylus. Victor Hugo.

III

DRAFT OF A PREFACE FOR THE Flowers of Evil

(To be combined perhaps with earlier notes)

If there is any glory in not being understood, or in being only very slightly so, I may without boasting say that with this little book I have at a single stroke both won and deserved that glory. Submitted several times over to various publishers who rejected it with disgust, put on trial and mutilated in 1857 as a result of a quite bizarre misapprehension, then gradually revived, augmented, and fortified during several years' silence, only to disappear again thanks to my losing interest, this discordant product of the Muse of modern times, again enlivened with a few violent new touches, dares today for the third time to face the sun of stupidity.

This is not my fault, but that of an insistent publisher who thinks he is strong enough to brave the public distaste. "This book will remain a stain on your whole life," one of my friends, a great poet, predicted from the beginning. And indeed all my misadventures have so far justified him. But I have one of those unhappy characters that enjoy hatred and feel glorified by contempt. My diabolically passionate taste for stupidity makes me take peculiar pleasure in the falsifications of calumny. Being as chaste as paper, as sober as water, as devout as a woman at communion, as harmless as a sacrificial lamb, it would not displease me to be taken for a debauchee, a drunkard, and infidel, a murderer. My publisher insists that it might be of some use, to me and to him, to explain why and how I have written this book, what were my means and aims, my plan and method. Such a critical task might well have the luck to interest those minds that love profound rhetoric. For those I shall perhaps write it later on and have it printed in ten copies. But, on second thought, doesn't it seem more obvious that this would be a quite superfluous undertaking for everyone concerned since those are the minds that already know or guess and the rest will never understand? I have too much fear of being ridiculous to wish to breath into the mass of humanity the understanding of my art object; in doing so, I should fear to resemble those Utopians who by decree wish to make all Frenchmen rich and virtuous at a single stroke. And moreover, my best, my supreme reason is that is annoys and bores me. Do we invite the crowd, the audience, behind the scenes, into the workshops of the costume and scene designers; into the actress's dressing room? Do we show the public (enthusiastic today, tomorrow indifferent) the mechanism behind our effects? Do we explain to them the revisions, the improvisations adopted in rehearsal, and even to what extent instinct and sincerity are mixed with artifice and charlatanry, all indispensable to the amalgam that is the work itself? Do we display all the rags, the rouge, the pulleys, the chains, the alterations, the scribbled-over proof sheets, in short all the horrors that make up the sanctuary of art?

In any case, such is not my mood today. I have no desire either to demonstrate, to astonish, to amuse, or to persuade. I have my nerves and my vertigo. I aspire to absolute rest and continuous night. Though I have sung the mad pleasures of wine and opium, I thirst only for a liqueur unknown on earth, which the pharmaceutics of heaven itself cannot afford me; a liquor that contains neither vitality nor death, neither excitation or extinction. To know nothing, to teach nothing, to will nothing, to feel nothing, to sleep and still to sleep, this today is my only wish. A base and loathsome wish, but sincere.

Nevertheless, since the best of taste teaches us not to fear contradicting ourselves a bit, I have collected at the end of this abominable book certain testimonials of sympathy from a few of the men I prize most, so that an impartial reader may infer from them that I am not absolutely deserving of excommunication, and that since I have managed to make myself loved of some, my heart, whatever printed rag may have said of it, is perhaps not "as frightfully hideous as my face."

Finally, the uncommon generosity which those gentlemen, the critics...

Since ignorance is increasing...

I take it on myself to denounce imitations...

(Translated by J.M.)

TO THE READER

Folly and error, avarice and vice,
Employ our souls and waste our bodies' force.
As mangy beggars incubate their lice,
We nourish our innocuous remorse.

Our sins are stubborn, craven our repentance.
For our week vows we ask excessive prices.
Trusting our tears will wash away the sentence,
We sneak off where the muddy road entices.

Cradled in evil, that Thrice-Great Magician,
The Devil, rocks our souls, that can't resist;
And the rich metal of our own volition
Is vaporized by that sage alchemist.

The Devil pulls the strings by which we're worked:
By all revolting objects lured, we slink
Hellwards; each day down one more step we're jerked
Feeling no horror, through the shades that stink.

Just as a lustful pauper bites and kisses
The scarred and shriveled breast of an old whore,
We steal, along the roadside, furtive blisses,
Squeezing them like stale oranges for more.

Packed tight, like hives of maggots, thickly seething,
Within our brains a host of demons surges.
Deep down into our lungs at every breathing,
Death flows, and unseen river, moaning dirges.

If rape or arson, poison, or the knife
Has wove no pleasing patterns in the stuff

Of this drab canvas we accept as life--
It is because we are not bold enough!

Amongst the jackals, leopards, mongrels, apes,
Snakes, scorpions, vultures, that with hellish din,
Squeal, roar, writhe, gambol, crawl, with monstrous shapes,
In each man's foul menagerie of sin--

There's one more damned than all. He never gambols,
Nor crawls, nor roars, but, from the rest withdrawn,
Gladly of this whole earth would make a shambles
And swallow up existence with a yawn...

Boredom! He smokes his hookah, while he dreams
Of gibbets, weeping tears he cannot smother.
You know this dainty monster, too, it seems--
Hypocrite reader! -- You! -- My twin! --My brother!

The Flowers of Evil

Benediction

When by the changeless Power of a Supreme Decree
The poet issues forth upon this sorry sphere,
His mother, horrified, and full of blasphemy,
Uplifts her voice to God, who takes compassion on her.

"Ah, why did I not bear a serpent's nest entire,
Instead of bringing forth this hideous Child of Doom!
Oh cursèd be that transient night of vain desire
When I conceived my expiation in my womb!"

"Yet since among all women thou hast chosen me
To be the degradation of my jaded mate,
And since I cannot like a love-leaf wantonly
Consign this stunted monster to the glowing grate,"

"I'll cause thine overwhelming hatred to rebound
Upon the cursèd tool of thy most wicked spite.
Forsooth, the branches of this wretched tree I'll wound
And rob its pestilential blossoms of their might!"

So thus, she giveth vent unto her foaming ire,
And knowing not the changeless statutes of all times,
Herself, amid the flames of hell, prepares the pyre;
The consecrated penance of maternal crimes.

Yet 'neath th' invisible shelter of an Angel's wing
This sunlight-loving infant disinherited,
Exhales from all he eats and drinks, and everything
The ever sweet ambrosia and the nectar red.

He trifles with the winds and with the clouds that glide,
About the way unto the Cross, he loves to sing,
The spirit on his pilgrimage; that faithful guide,
Oft weeps to see him joyful like a bird of Spring.

All those that he would cherish shrink from him with fear,
And some that waxen bold by his tranquility,
Endeavour hard some grievance from his heart to tear,

And make on him the trial of their ferocity.

Within the bread and wine outspread for his repast
To mingle dust and dirty spittle they essay,
And everything he touches, forth they slyly cast,
Or scourge themselves, if e'er their feet betrod his way.

His wife goes round proclaiming in the crowded quads--
"Since he can find my body beauteous to behold,
Why not perform the office of those ancient gods
And like unto them, redeck myself with shining gold?"

"I'll bathe myself with incense, spikenard and myrrh,
With genuflexions, delicate viandes and wine,
To see, in jest, if from a heart, that loves me dear,
I cannot filch away the hommages divine."

"And when of these impious jokes at length I tire,
My frail but mighty hands, around his breast entwined,
With nails, like harpies' nails, shall cunningly conspire
The hidden path unto his feeble heart to find."

"And like a youngling bird that trembles in its nest,
I'll pluck his heart right out; within its own blood drowned,
And finally to satiate my favourite beast,
I'll throw it with intense disdain upon the ground!"

Towards the Heavens where he sees the sacred grail
The poet calmly stretches forth his pious arms,
Whereon the lightenings from his lucid spirit veil
The sight of the infuriated mob that swarms.

"Oh blest be thou, Almighty who bestowest pain,
Like some divine redress for our infirmities,
And like the most refreshing and the purest rain,
To sanctify the strong, for saintly ecstasies."

"I know that for the poet thou wilt grant a chair,
Among the Sainted Legion and the Blissful ones,
That of the endless feast thou wilt accord his share
To him, of Virtues, Dominations and of Thrones."

11

"I know, that Sorrow is that nobleness alone,
 Which never may corrupted be by hell nor curse,
 I know, in order to enwreathe my mystic crown
 I must inspire the ages and the universe."

"And yet the buried jewels of Palmyra old,
 The undiscovered metals and the pearly sea
 Of gems, that unto me you show could never hold
 Beside this diadem of blinding brilliancy."

"For it shall be engendered from the purest fire
 Of rays primeval, from the holy hearth amassed,
 Of which the eyes of Mortals, in their sheen entire,
 Are but the tarnished mirrors, sad and overcast!"

Echoes

In Nature's temple, living columns rise,
Which oftentimes give tongue to words subdued,
And Man traverses this symbolic wood,
Which looks at him with half familiar eyes,

Like lingering echoes, which afar confound
Themselves in deep and sombre unity,
As vast as Night, and like transplendency,
The scents and colours to each other respond.

And scents there are, like infant's flesh as chaste,
As sweet as oboes, and as meadows fair,
And others, proud, corrupted, rich and vast,

Which have the expansion of infinity,
Like amber, musk and frankincense and myrrh,
That sing the soul's and senses' ecstasy.

The Sick Muse

Alas--my poor Muse--what aileth thee now?
Thine eyes are bedimmed with the visions of Night,
And silent and cold--I perceive on thy brow
In their turns--Despair and Madness alight.

A succubus green, or a hobgoblin red,
Has it poured o'er thee Horror and Love from its urn?
Or the Nightmare with masterful bearing hath led
Thee to drown in the depths of some magic Minturne?

I wish, as the health-giving fragrance I cull,
That thy breast with strong thoughts could for ever be full,
And that rhymthmic'ly flowing--thy Christian blood

Could resemble the olden-time metrical-flood,
Where each in his turn reigned the father of Rhymes
Phoebus--and Pan, lord of Harvest-times.

The Venal Muse

Oh Muse of my heart--so fond of palaces old,
Wilt have--when New Year speeds its wintry blast,
Amid those tedious nights, with snow o'ercast,
A log to warm thy feet, benumbed with cold?

Wilt thou thy marbled shoulders then revive
With nightly rays that through thy shutters peep?
And--void thy purse and void thy palace--reap
A golden hoard within some azure hive?

Thou must, to earn thy daily bread, each night,
Suspend the censer like an acolyte,

13

Te-Deums sing, with sanctimonious ease,

Or as a famished mountebank, with jokes obscene
Essay to lull the vulgar rabble's spleen;
Thy laughter soaked in tears which no one sees.

The Evil Monk

The cloisters old, expounded on their walls
With paintings, the Beatic Verity,
The which--adorning their religious halls,
Enriched the frigidness of their Austerity.

In days when Christian seeds bloomed o'er the land,
Full many a noble monk unknown to-day,
Upon the field of tombs would take his stand,
Exalting Death in rude and simple way.

My soul is a tomb where--bad monk that I be--
I dwell and search its depths from all eternity,
And nought bedecks the walls of the odious spot.

Oh sluggard monk! when shall I glean aright
From the living spectacle of my bitter lot,
To mold my handywork and mine eyes' Delight?

The Enemy

My childhood was nought but a ravaging storm,
Enlivened at times by a brilliant sun;
The rain and the winds wrought such havoc and harm
That of buds on my plot there remains hardly one.

Behold now the Fall of ideas I have reached,
And the shovel and rake one must therefore resume,

In collecting the turf, inundated and breached,
Where the waters dug trenches as deep as a tomb.

And yet these new blossoms, for which I craved,
Will they find in this earth--like a shore that is laved--
The mystical fuel which vigour imparts?

Oh misery!--Time devours our lives,
And the enemy black, which consumeth our hearts
On the blood of our bodies, increases and thrives!

Ill Luck

This heavy burden to uplift,
O Sysiphus, thy pluck is required!
And even though the heart aspired,
Art is long and Time is swift.

Afar from sepulchres renowned,
To a graveyard, quite apart,
Like a broken drum, my heart,
Beats the funeral marches' sound.

Many a buried jewel sleeps
In the long-forgotten deeps,
Far from mattock and from sound;

Many a flower wafts aloft
Its perfumes, like a secret soft,
Within the solitudes, profound.

Interior Life

A long while I dwelt beneath vast porticoes,
While the ocean-suns bathed with a thousand fires,
And which with their great and majestic spires,
At eventide looked like basaltic grottoes.

The billows, in rolling depictured the skies,
And mingled, in solemn and mystical strain,
The all-mighteous chords of their luscious refrain
With the sun-set's colours reflexed in mine eyes.

It is there that I lived in exalted calm,
In the midst of the azure, the splendour, the waves,
While pregnant with perfumes, naked slaves

Refreshed my forehead with branches of palm,
Whose gentle and only care was to know
The secret that caused me to languish so.

Man and the Sea

Free man! the sea is to thee ever dear!
The sea is thy mirror, thou regardest thy soul
In its mighteous waves that unendingly roll,
And thy spirit is yet not a chasm less drear.

Thou delight'st to plunge deep in thine image down;
Thou tak'st it with eyes and with arms in embrace,
And at times thine own inward voice would'st efface
With the sound of its savage ungovernable moan.

You are both of you, sombre, secretive and deep:
Oh mortal, thy depths are foraye unexplored,
Oh sea--no one knoweth thy dazzling hoard,
You both are so jealous your secrets to keep!

And endless ages have wandered by,
Yet still without pity or mercy you fight,
So mighty in plunder and death your delight:
Oh wrestlers! so constant in enmity!

Beauty

I am lovely, O mortals, like a dream of stone,
And my bosom, where each one gets bruised in turn,
To inspire the love of a poet is prone,
Like matter eternally silent and stern.

As an unfathomed sphinx, enthroned by the Nile,
My heart a swan's whiteness with granite combines,
And I hate every movement, displacing the lines,
And never I weep and never I smile.

The poets in front of mine attitudes fine
(Which the proudest of monuments seem to implant),
To studies profound all their moments assign,

For I have all these docile swains to enchant--
Two mirrors, which Beauty in all things ignite:
Mine eyes, my large eyes, of eternal Light!

The Ideal

It could ne'er be those beauties of ivory vignettes;
The varied display of a worthless age,
Nor puppet-like figures with castonets,
That ever an heart like mine could engage.

I leave to Gavarni, that poet of chlorosis,

His hospital-beauties in troups that whirl,
For I cannot discover amid his pale roses
A flower to resemble my scarlet ideal.

Since, what for this fathomless heart I require
Is--Lady Macbeth you! in crime so dire;
--An Æschylus dream transposed from the South--

Or thee, oh great "Night" of Michael-Angelo born,
Who so calmly thy limbs in strange posture hath drawn,
Whose allurements are framed for a Titan's mouth.

The Giantess

I should have loved--erewhile when Heaven conceived
Each day, some child abnormal and obscene,
Beside a maiden giantess to have lived,
Like a luxurious cat at the feet of a queen;

To see her body flowering with her soul,
And grow, unchained, in awe-inspiring art,
Within the mists across her eyes that stole
To divine the fires entombed within her heart.

And oft to scramble o'er her mighty limbs,
And climb the slopes of her enormous knees,
Or in summer when the scorching sunlight streams

Across the country, to recline at ease,
And slumber in the shadow of her breast
Like an hamlet 'neath the mountain-crest.

Hymn to Beauty

O Beauty! dost thou generate from Heaven or from Hell?
Within thy glance, so diabolic and divine,
Confusedly both wickedness and goodness dwell,
And hence one might compare thee unto sparkling wine.

Thy look containeth both the dawn and sunset stars,
Thy perfumes, as upon a sultry night exhale,
Thy kiss a philter, and thy mouth a Grecian vase,
That renders heroes cowardly and infants hale.

Yea, art thou from the planets, or the fiery womb?
The demon follows in thy train, with magic fraught,
Thou scatter'st seeds haphazardly of joy and doom,
Thou govern'st everything, but answer'st unto nought.

O Loveliness! thou spurnest corpses with delight,
Among thy jewels, Horror hath such charms for thee,
And Murder 'mid thy mostly cherished trinklets bright,
Upon thy massive bosom dances amorously.

The blinded, fluttering moth towards the candle flies,
Then frizzles, falls, and falters--"Blessings unto thee"--
The panting swain that o'er his beauteous mistress sighs,
Seems like the Sick, that stroke their gravestones lovingly.

What matter, if thou comest from the Heavens or Hell,
O Beauty, frightful ghoul, ingenuous and obscure!
So long thine eyes, thy smile, to me the way can tell
Towards that Infinite I love, but never saw.

From God or Satan? Angel, Mermaid, Proserpine?
What matter if thou makest--blithe, voluptuous sprite--
With rhythms, perfumes, visions--O mine only queen!--
The universe less hideous and the hours less trite.

Exotic Perfume

When, with closed eyes, on a hot afternoon,
The scent of thine ardent breast I inhale,
Celestial vistas my spirit assail;
Caressed by the flames of an endless sun.

A langorous island, where Nature abounds
With exotic trees and luscious fruit;
And with men whose bodies are slim and astute,
And with women whose frankness delights and astounds.

By thy perfume enticed to this region remote,
A port I see, laden with mast and with boat,
Still wearied and torn by the distant brine;

While the tamarisk-odours that dreamily throng
The air, round my slumberous senses intwine,
And mix, in my soul, with the mariners' song.

La Chevelure

O fleece, that foams down unto the shoulders bare!
O curls, O scents which lovely languidness exhale!
Delight! to fill this alcove's sombre atmosphere
With memories, sleeping deep within this tress of hair,
I'll wave it in the evening breezes like a veil!

The shores of Africa, and Asia's burning skies,
A world forgotten, distant, nearly dead and spent,
Within thy depths, O aromatic forest! lies.
And like to spirits floating unto melodies,
Mine own, Belovèd! glides within thy sacred scent.

There I will hasten, where the trees and humankind
With languor lull beside the hot and silent sea;
Strong tresses bear me, be to me the waves and wind!

Within thy fragrance lies a dazzling dream confined
Of sails and masts and flames--O lake of ebony!

A loudly echoing harbour, where my soul may hold
To quaff, the silver cup of colours, scents and sounds,
Wherein the vessels glide upon a sea of gold,
And stretch their mighty arms, the glory to enfold
Of virgin skies, where never-ending heat abounds.

I'll plunge my brow, enamoured with voluptuousness
Within this darkling ocean of infinitude,
Until my subtle spirit, which thy waves caress,
Shall find you once again, O fertile weariness;
Unending lullabye of perfumed lassitude!

Ye tresses blue--recess of strange and sombre shades,
Ye make the azure of the starry Realm immense;
Upon the downy beeches, by your curls' cascades,
Among your mingling fragrances, my spirit wades
To cull the musk and cocoa-nut and lotus scents.

Long--foraye--my hand, within thy heavy mane,
Shall scatter rubies, pearls, sapphires eternally,
And thus my soul's desire for thee shall never wane;
For art not thou the oasis where I dream and drain
With draughts profound, the golden wine of memory?

Sonnet XXVIII

With pearly robes that wave within the wind,
Even when she walks, she seems to dance,
Like swaying serpents round those wands entwined
Which fakirs ware in rhythmic elegance.

So like the desert's Blue, and the sands remote,
Both, deaf to mortal suffering and to strife,
Or like the sea-weeds 'neath the waves that float,
Indifferently she moulds her budding life.

Her polished eyes are made of minerals bright,
And in her mien, symbolical and cold,
Wherein an angel mingles with a sphinx of old,

Where all is gold, and steel, and gems, and light,
There shines, just like a useless star eternally,
The sterile woman's frigid majesty.

Posthumous Remorse

Ah, when thou shalt slumber, my darkling love,
Beneath a black marble-made statuette,
And when thou'lt have nought for thy house or alcove,
But a cavernous den and a damp oubliette.

When the tomb-stone, oppressing thy timorous breast,
And thy hips drooping sweetly with listless decay,
The pulse and desires of mine heart shall arrest,
And thy feet from pursuing their adventurous way,

Then the grave, that dark friend of my limitless dreams
(For the grave ever readeth the poet aright),
Amid those long nights, which no slumber redeems

'Twill query--"What use to thee, incomplete spright
That thou ne'er hast unfathomed the tears of the dead"?--
Then the worms will gnaw deep at thy body, like Dread.

The Balcony

Oh, Mother of Memories! Mistress of Mistresses!
Oh, thou all my pleasures, oh, thou all my prayers!
Can'st thou remember those luscious caresses,
The charm of the hearth and the sweet evening airs?

Oh, Mother, of Memories, Mistress of Mistresses!

Those evenings illumed by the glow of the coal,
And those roseate nights with their vaporous wings,
How calm was thy breast and how good was thy soul,
'Twas then we uttered imperishable things,
Those evenings illumed by the glow of the coal.

How lovely the suns on those hot, autumn nights!
How vast were the heavens! and the heart how hale!
As I leaned towards you--oh, my Queen of Delights,
The scent of thy blood I seemed to inhale.
How lovely the sun on those hot, autumn nights!

The shadows of night-time grew dense like a pall,
And deep through the darkness thine eyes I divined,
And I drank of thy breath--oh sweetness, oh gall,
And thy feet in my brotherly hands reclined,
The shadows of Night-time grew dense like a pall.

I know how to call forth those moments so dear,
And to live my Past--laid on thy knees--once more,
For where should I seek for thy beauties but here
In thy langorous heart and thy body so pure?
I know how to call forth those moments so dear.

Those perfumes, those infinite kisses and sighs,
Are they born in some gulf to our plummets denied?
Like rejuvenate suns that mount up to the skies,
That first have been cleansed in the depths of the tide;
Oh, perfumes! oh, infinite kisses and sighs!

The Possessed One

The sun is enveloped in crape! like it,
O Moon of my Life! wrap thyself up in shade;
At will, smoke or slumber, be silent, be staid,
And dive deep down in Dispassion's dark pit.

I cherish thee thus! But if 'tis thy mood,
Like a star that from out its penumbra appears,
To float in the regions where madness careers,
Fair dagger! burst forth from thy sheath! 'tis good.

Yea, light up thine eyes at the Fire of Renown!
Or kindle desire by the looks of some clown!
Thine All is my joy, whether dull or aflame!

Just be what thou wilt, black night, dawn divine,
There is not a nerve in my trembling frame
But cries, "I adore thee, Beelzebub mine!"

Semper Eadem

"From whence it comes, you ask, this gloom acute,
Like waves that o'er the rocky headland fall?"
--When once our hearts have gathered in their fruit,
To live is a curse! a secret known to all,

A grief, quite simple, nought mysterious,
And like your joy--for all, both loud and shrill,
Nay cease to clamour, be not e'er so curious!
And yet although your voice is sweet, be still!

Be still, O soul, with rapture ever rife!
O mouth, with the childish smile! Far more than Life,
The subtle bonds of Death around us twine.

Let--let my heart, the wine of falsehood drink,
And dream-like, deep within your fair eyes sink,
And in the shade of thy lashes long recline!

All Entire

The Demon, in my lofty vault,
This morning came to visit me,
And striving me to find at fault,
He said, "Fain would I know of thee;

"Among the many beauteous things,
--All which _her_ subtle grace proclaim--
Among the dark and rosy things,
Which go to make her charming frame,

"Which is the sweetest unto thee"?
My soul! to Him thou didst retort--
"Since all with her is destiny,
Of preference there can be nought.

When all transports me with delight,
If aught deludes I can not know,
She either lulls one like the Night,
Or dazzles like the Morning-glow.

That harmony is too divine,
Which governs all her body fair,
For powerless mortals to define
In notes the many concords there.

O mystic metamorphosis
Of all my senses blent in one!
Her voice a beauteous perfume is,
Her breath makes music, chaste and wan.

Sonnet XLIII

What sayest thou, to-night, poor soul so drear,
What sayest--heart erewhile engulfed in gloom,
To the very lovely, very chaste, and very dear,
Whose god-like look hath made thee to re-bloom?

To her, with pride we chant an echoing Hymn,
For nought can touch the sweetness of her sway;
Her flesh ethereal as the seraphim,
Her eyes with robe of light our souls array.

And be it in the night, or solitude,
Among the streets or 'mid the multitude,
Her shadow, torch-like, dances in the air,

And murmurs, "I, the Beautiful proclaim--
That for my sake, alone ye love the Fair;
I am the Guardian Angel, Muse and Dame!"

The Living Torch

They stand before me now, those eyes that shine,
No doubt inspired by an Angel wise;
They stand, those God-like brothers that are mine,
And pour their diamond fires in mine eyes.

From all transgressions, from all snares, they save,
Towards the Path of Joy they guide my ways;
They are my servants, and I am their slave;
And all my soul, this living torch obeys.

Ye charming Eyes--ye have those mystic beams,
Of candles, burning in full day; the sun
Awakes, yet kills not their fantastic gleams:

Ye sing the Awak'ning, they the dark oblivion;
The Awak'ning of my spirit ye proclaim,
O stars--no sun can ever kill your flame!

The Spiritual Dawn

When the morning white and rosy breaks,
With the gnawing Ideal, upon the debauchee,
By the power of a strange decree,
Within the sotted beast an Angel wakes.

The mental Heaven's inaccessible blue,
For wearied mortals that still dream and mourn,
Expands and sinks; towards the chasm drawn.
Thus, cherished goddess, Being pure and true--

Upon the rests of foolish orgy-nights
Thine image, more sublime, more pink, more clear,
Before my staring eyes is ever there.

The sun has darkened all the candle lights;
And thus thy spectre like the immortal sun,
Is ever victorious--thou resplendent one!

Evening Harmony

The hour approacheth, when, as their stems incline,
The flowers evaporate like an incense urn,
And sounds and scents in the vesper breezes turn;
A melancholy waltz--and a drowsiness divine.

The flowers evaporate like an incense urn,
The viol vibrates like the wailing of souls that repine.
A melancholy waltz--and a drowsiness divine,

The skies like a mosque are beautiful and stern.

The viol vibrates like the wailing of souls that repine;
Sweet souls that shrink from chaos vast and etern,
The skies like a mosque are beautiful and stern,
The sunset drowns within its blood-red brine.

Sweet souls that shrink from chaos vast and etern,
Essay the wreaths of their faded Past to entwine,
The sunset drowns within its blood-red brine,
Thy thought within me glows like an incense urn.

Overcast Sky

Meseemeth thy glance, soft enshrouded with dew,
Thy mysterious eyes (are they grey, green or blue?),
Alternately cruel, and tender, and shy,
Reflect both the languor and calm of the sky.

Thou recall est those white days--with shadows caressed,
Engendering tears from th' enraptured breast,
When racked by an anguish unfathomed that weeps,
The nerves, too awake, jibe the spirit that sleeps.

At times--thou art like those horizons divine,
Where the suns of the nebulous seasons decline;
How resplendent art thou--O pasturage vast,
Illumed by the beams of a sky overcast!

O! dangerous dame--oh seductive clime!
As well, will I love both thy snow and thy rime,
And shall I know how from the frosts to entice
Delights that are keener than iron and ice?

Invitation to a Journey

My sister, my dear
Consider how fair,
Together to live it would be!
Down yonder to fly
To love, till we die,
In the land which resembles thee.
Those suns that rise
'Neath erratic skies,
--No charm could be like unto theirs--
So strange and divine,
Like those eyes of thine
Which glow in the midst of their tears.

There, all is order and loveliness,
Luxury, calm and voluptuousness.

The tables and chairs,
Polished bright by the years,
Would decorate sweetly our rooms,
And the rarest of flowers
Would twine round our bowers
And mingle their amber perfumes:
The ceilings arrayed,
And the mirrors inlaid,
This Eastern splendour among,
Would furtively steal
O'er our souls, and appeal
With its tranquillous native tongue.

There, all is order and loveliness,
Luxury, calm and voluptuousness.

In the harbours, peep,
At the vessels asleep
(Their humour is always to roam),
Yet it is but to grant
Thy smallest want

From the ends of the earth that they come,
 The sunsets beam
 Upon meadow and stream,
And upon the city entire
 'Neath a violet crest,
 The world sinks to rest,
Illumed by a golden fire.

There, all is order and loveliness,
Luxury, calm and voluptuousness.

"Causerie"

You are a roseate autumn-sky, that glows!
Yet sadness rises in me like the flood,
And leaves in ebbing on my lips morose,
The poignant memory of its bitter mind.

In vain your hands my swooning breast embrace,
Oh, friend! alone remains the plundered spot,
Where woman's biting grip has left its trace:
My heart, the beasts devoured--seek it not!

My heart is a palace pillaged by the herd;
They kill and take each other by the throat!
A perfume glides around your bosom bared--

O loveliness, thou scourge of souls--devote
Thine eyes of fire--luminous-like feasts,
To burn these rags--rejected by the beasts!

Autumn Song

I

Shortly we will plunge within the frigid gloom,
Farewell swift summer brightness; all too short--
I hear already sounding with a death-like boom
The wood that falls upon the pavement of the court.

The whole of winter enters in my Being--pain,
Hate, honor, labour hard and forced--and dread,
And like the northern sun upon its polar plane
My heart will soon be but a stone, iced and red.

I listen trembling unto every log that falls,
The scaffold, which they build, has not a duller sound,
My spirits waver, like the trembling tower walls
that shake--with every echoing blow the builders pound.

Meeseemeth--as to these monotonous blows I sway,
They nail for one a coffin lid, or sound a knell--
For whom? Autumn now--and summer yesterday!
This strange mysterious noise betokens a farewell.

II

I love within your oblong eyes the verdant rays,
My sweet! but bitter everything to-day meseems:
And nought--your love, the boudoir, nor the flickering blaze,
Can replace the sun that o'er the screen streams.

And yet bemother and caress me, tender heart!
Even me the thankless and the worthless one;
Beloved or sister--unto me the sweets impart
Of a glorious autumn or a sinking sun.

Ephemeral task! the beckoning the beckoning empty tomb is set!

Oh grant me--as upon your knees my head I lay,
(Because the white and torrid summer I regret),
To taste the parted season's mild and amber ray.

Sisina

Imagine Diana in gorgeous array,
How into the forests and thickets she flies,
With her hair in the breezes, and flushed for the fray,
How the very best riders she proudly defies.

Have you seen Théroigne, of the blood-thirsty heart,
As an unshod herd to attack he bestirs,
With cheeks all inflamed, playing up to his part,
As he goes, sword in hand, up the royal stairs?

And so is Sisina--yet this warrior sweet,
Has a soul with compassion and kindness replete,
Inspired by drums and by powder, her sway

Knows how to concede to the supplicants' prayers,
And her bosom, laid waste by the flames, has alway,
For those that are worthy, a fountain of tears.

To a Creolean Lady

In a country perfumed with the sun's embrace,
I knew 'neath a dais of purpled palms,
And branches where idleness weeps o'er one's face,
A Creolean lady of unknown charms.

Her tint, pale and warm--this bewitching bride,
Displays a nobly nurtured mien,
Courageous and grand like a huntsman, her stride;
A tranquil smile and eyes serene.

If, madam, you'd go to the true land of gain,
By the banks of the verdant Loire or the Seine,
How worthy to garnish some pile of renown.

You'd awake in the calm of some shadowy nest,
A thousand songs in the poet's breast,
That your eyes would inspire far more than your brown.

Moesta et Errabunda

Oh, Agatha, tell! does thy heart not at times fly away?
Far from the city impure and the lowering sea,
To another ocean that blinds with its dazzling array,
So blue and so clear and profound, like virginity?
Oh, Agatha, tell! does thy heart not at times fly away?

The sea, the vast ocean our travail and trouble consoles!
What demon hath gifted the sea with a voice from on high,
To sing us (attuned to an Æolus-organ that rolls
Forth a grumbling burden) a lenitive lullabye?
The sea, the vast ocean our travail and trouble consoles!

Oh, carry me, waggons, oh, sailing-ships, help me depart!
Far, far, here the dust is quite wet with our showering tears,
Oh, say! it is true that Agatha's desolate heart,
Proclaimeth, "Away from remorse, and from crimes, and from cares,"
Oh, carry me, waggons, oh, sailing ships, help me depart!

How distant you seem to be, perfumed Elysian fields!
Wherein there is nothing but sunshine and love and glee;
Where all that one loves is so worthy, and lovingly yields,
And our hearts float about in the purest of ecstasy,
How distant you seem to be, perfumed Elysian fields!

But the green paradise of those transient infantile loves,
The strolls, and the songs, and the kisses, and bunches of flowers,
The viols vibrating beyond, in the mountainous groves,

With the chalice of wine and the evening, entwined, in the bowers,
But the green paradise of those transient infantile loves.

That innocent heaven o'erflowing with furtive delight,
Than China or India, is it still further away?
Or, could one with pityful prayers bring it back to our sight?
Or yet with a silvery voice o'er the ages convey
That innocent heaven o'erflowing with furtive delight!

The Ghost

Just like an angel with evil eye,
I shall return to thee silently,
Upon thy bower I'll alight,
With falling shadows of the night.

With thee, my brownie, I'll commune,
And give thee kisses cold as the moon,
And with a serpent's moist embrace,
I'll crawl around thy resting-place.

And when the livid morning falls,
Thou'lt find alone the empty walls,
And till the evening, cold 'twill be.

As others with their tenderness,
Upon thy life and youthfulness,
I'll reign alone with dread o'er thee.

Autumn Song

They ask me--thy crystalline eyes, so acute,
"Odd lover--why am I to thee so dear?"
--Be sweet and keep silent, my heart, which is sear,
For all save the rude and untutored brute,

Is loth its infernal depths to reveal,
And its dissolute motto engraven with fire,
Oh charmer! whose arms endless slumber inspire!
I abominate passion and wit makes me ill.

So let us love gently. Within his retreat,
Foreboding, Love seeks for his arrows a prey,
I know all the arms of his battle array.

Delirium and loathing--O pale Marguerite!
Like me, art thou not an autumnal ray,
Alas my so white, my so cold Marguerite!

Sadness of the Moon-Goddess

To-night the Moon dreams with increased weariness,
Like a beauty stretched forth on a downy heap
Of rugs, while her languorous fingers caress
The contour of her breasts, before falling to sleep.

On the satin back of the avalanche soft,
She falls into lingering swoons, as she dies,
While she lifteth her eyes to white visions aloft,
Which like efflorescence float up to the skies.

When at times, in her languor, down on to this sphere,
She slyly lets trickle a furtive tear,
A poet, desiring slumber to shun,

Takes up this pale tear in the palm of his hand
(The colours of which like an opal blend),
And buries it far from the eyes of the sun.

Cats

All ardent lovers and all sages prize,
--As ripening years incline upon their brows--
The mild and mighty cats--pride of the house--
That like unto them are indolent, stern and wise.

The friends of Learning and of Ecstasy,
They search for silence and the horrors of gloom;
The devil had used them for his steeds of Doom,
Could he alone have bent their pride to slavery.

When musing, they display those outlines chaste,
Of the great sphinxes--stretched o'er the sandy waste,
That seem to slumber deep in a dream without end:

From out their loins a fountainous furnace flies,
And grains of sparkling gold, as fine as sand,
Bestar the mystic pupils of their eyes.

Owls

Beneath the shades of sombre yews,
The silent owls sit ranged in rows,
Like ancient idols, strangely pose,
And darting fiery eyes, they muse.

Immovable, they sit and gaze,
Until the melancholy hour,
At which the darknesses devour
The faded sunset's slanting rays.

Their attitude, instructs the wise,
That he--within this world--who flies
From tumult and from merriment;

36

The man allured by a passing face,
For ever bears the chastisement
Of having wished to change his place.

Music

Oft Music possesses me like the seas!
  To my planet pale,
'Neath a ceiling of mist, in the lofty breeze,
  I set my sail.

With inflated lungs and expanded chest,
  Like to a sail,
On the backs of the heaped-up billows I rest--
  Which the shadows veil--

I feel all the anguish within me arise
  Of a ship in distress;
The tempest, the rain, 'neath the lowering skies,

  My body caress;
At times, the calm pool or the mirror clear
  Of my despair!

The Joyous Defunct

Where snails abound--in a juicy soil,
I will dig for myself a fathomless grave,
Where at leisure mine ancient bones I can coil,
And sleep--quite forgotten--like a shark 'neath the wave.

I hate every tomb--I abominate wills,
And rather than tears from the world to implore,

I would ask of the crows with their vampire bills
To devour every bit of my carcass impure.

Oh worms, without eyes, without ears, black friends!
To you a defunct-one, rejoicing, descends,
Enlivened Philosophers--offspring of Dung!

Without any qualms, o'er my wreckage spread,
And tell if some torment there still can be wrung
For this soul-less old frame that is dead 'midst the dead!

The Broken Bell

How sweet and bitter, on a winter night,
Beside the palpitating fire to list,
As, slowly, distant memories alight,
To sounds of chimes that sing across the mist.

Oh, happy is that bell with hearty throat,
Which neither age nor time can e'er defeat,
Which faithfully uplifts its pious note,
Like an agèd soldier on his beat.

For me, my soul is cracked, and 'mid her cares,
Would often fill with her songs the midnight airs
And oft it chances that her feeble moan

Is like the wounded warrior's fainting groan,
Who by a lake of blood, 'neath bodies slain,
In anguish falls, and never moves again.

Spleen

The rainy moon of all the world is weary,
And from its urn a gloomy cold pours down,
Upon the pallid inmates of the mortuary,
And on the neighbouring outskirts of the town.

My wasted cat, in searching for a litter,
Bestirs its mangy paws from post to post;
(A poet's soul that wanders in the gutter,
With the jaded voice of a shiv'ring ghost).

The smoking pine-log, while the drone laments,
Accompanies the wheezy pendulum,
The while amidst a haze of dirty scents,

--Those fatal remnants of a sick man's room--
The gallant knave of hearts and queen of spades
Relate their ancient amorous escapades.

Obsession

Great forests, you alarm me like a mighty fane;
Like organ-tones you roar, and in our hearts of stone,
Where ancient sobs vibrate, O halls of endless pain!
The answering echoes of your "De Profundis" moan.

I hate thee, Ocean! hate thy tumults and thy throbs,
My spirit finds them in himself. This bitter glee
Of vanquished mortals, full of insults and of sobs,
I hear it in the mighteous laughter of the sea.

O starless night! thy loveliness my soul inhales,
Without those starry rays which speak a language known,
For I desire the dark, the naked and the lone.

But e'en those darknesses themselves to me are veils,
Where live--and, by the millions 'neath my eyelids prance,
Long, long departed Beings with familiar glance.

Magnetic Horror

"Beneath this sky, so livid and strange,
Tormented like thy destiny,
What thoughts within thy spirit range
Themselves?--O libertine reply."

--With vain desires, for ever torn
Towards the uncertain, and the vast,
And yet, like Ovid--I'll not mourn--
Who from his Roman Heaven was cast.

O heavens, turbulent as the streams,
In you I mirror forth my pride!
Your clouds, which clad in mourning, glide,

Are the hearses of my dreams,
And in your illusion lies the hell,
Wherein my heart delights to dwell.

The Lid

Where'er he may rove, upon sea or on land,
'Neath a fiery sky or a pallid sun,
Be he Christian or one of Cythera's band,
Opulent Croesus or beggar--'tis one,

Whether citizen, peasant or vagabond he,
Be his little brain active or dull. Everywhere,
Man feels the terror of mystery,

And looks upon high with a glance full of fear.

The Heaven above, that oppressive wall;
A ceiling lit up in some lewd music hall,
Where the actors step forth on a blood-red soil;

The eremite's hope, and the dread of the sot,
The Sky; that black lid of a mighty pot,
Where, vast and minute, human Races boil.

Bertha's Eyes

The loveliest eyes you can scorn with your wondrous glow:
O! beautiful childish eyes there abounds in your light,
A something unspeakably tender and good as the night:
O! eyes! over me your enchanting darkness let flow.

Large eyes of my child! O Arcana profoundly adored!
Ye resemble so closely those caves in the magical creek;
Where within the deep slumbering shade of some petrified peak,
There shines, undiscovered, the gems of a dazzling hoard.

My child has got eyes so profound and so dark and so vast,
Like thee! oh unending Night, and thy mystical shine:
Their flames are those thoughts that with Love and with Faith combine,
And sparkle deep down in the depths so alluring or chaste.

The Set of the Romantic Sun

How beauteous the sun as it rises supreme,
Like an explosion that greets us from above,
Oh, happy is he that can hail with love,
Its decline, more glorious far, than a dream.

I saw flower, furrow, and brook.... I recall
How they swooned like a tremulous heart 'neath the sun,
Let us haste to the sky-line, 'tis late, let us run,
At least to catch one slanting ray ere it fall.

But the god, who eludes me, I chase all in vain,
The night, irresistible, plants its domain,
Black mists and vague shivers of death it forbodes;

While an odour of graves through the darkness spreads,
And on the swamp's margin, my timid foot treads
Upon slimy snails, and on unseen toads.

Meditation

Be wise, O my Woe, seek thy grievance to drown,
Thou didst call for the night, and behold it is here,
An atmosphere sombre, envelopes the town,
To some bringing peace and to others a care.

Whilst the manifold souls of the vile multitude,
'Neath the lash of enjoyment, that merciless sway,
Go plucking remorse from the menial brood,
From them far, O my grief, hold my hand, come this way.

Behold how they beckon, those years, long expired,
From Heaven, in faded apparel attired,
How Regret, smiling, foams on the waters like yeast;

Its arches of slumber the dying sun spreads,
And like a long winding-sheet dragged to the East,
Oh, hearken Beloved, how the Night softly treads!

To a Passer-by

Around me thundered the deafening noise of the street,
In mourning apparel, portraying majestic distress,
With queenly fingers, just lifting the hem of her dress,
A stately woman passed by with hurrying feet.

Agile and noble, with limbs of perfect poise,
Ah, how I drank, thrilled through like a Being insane,
In her look, a dark sky, from whence springs forth the hurricane,
There lay but the sweetness that charms, and the joy that destroys.

A flash--then the night.... O loveliness fugitive!
Whose glance has so suddenly caused me again to live,
Shall I not see you again till this life is o'er!

Elsewhere, far away ... too late, perhaps never more,
For I know not whither you fly, nor you, where I go,
O soul that I would have loved, and _that_ you know!

Illusionary Love

When I behold thee wander by, my languorous love,
To songs of viols which throughout the dome resound,
Harmonious and stately as thy footsteps move,
Bestowing forth the languor of thy glance profound.

When I regard thee, glowing in the gaslight rays,
Thy pallid brow embellished by a charm obscure,
Here where the evening torches light the twilight haze,
Thine eyes attracting me like those of a portraiture,

I say--How beautiful she is! how strangely rich!
A mighty memory, royal and commanding tower,

A garland: and her heart, bruised like a ruddy peach,
Is ripe--like her body for Love's sapient power.

Art thou, that spicy Autumn-fruit with taste supreme?
Art thou a funeral vase inviting tears of grief?
Aroma--causing one of Eastern wastes to dream;
A downy cushion, bunch of flowers or golden sheaf?

I know that there are eyes, most melancholy ones,
Wherein no precious secret deeply hidden lies,
Resplendent shrines, devoid of relics, sacred stones,
More empty, more profound than ye yourselves, O skies?

Yea, does thy semblance, not alone for me suffice,
To kindle senses which the cruel truth abhor?
All one to me! thy folly or thy heart of ice,
Decoy or mask, all hail! thy beauty I adore!

Mists and Rains

O last of Autumn and Winter--steeped in haze,
O sleepy seasons! you I love and praise,
Because around my heart and brain you twine
A misty winding-sheet and a nebulous shrine.

On that great plain, where frigid blasts abound,
Where through the nights, so long, the vane whirls round,
My soul, more free than in the springtime soft,
Will stretch her raven wings and soar aloft,

Unto an heart with gloomy things replete,
On which remain the frosts of former Times,
O pallid seasons, mistress of our climes

As your pale shadows--nothing is so sweet,
Unless it be, on a moonless night a-twain,
On some chance couch to soothe to sleep our Pain.

The Wine of Lovers

To-day the Distance is superb,
Without bridle, spur or curb,
Let us mount on the back of wine
For Regions fairy and divine!

Let's, like two angels tortured by
Some dark, delirious phantasy,
Pursue the distant mirage drawn
O'er the blue crystal of the dawn!

And gently balanced on the wing
Of some obliging whirlwind, we
--In equal rapture revelling--

My sister, side by side will flee,
Without repose, nor truce, where gleams
The golden Paradise of my dreams!

Condemned Women

Like thoughtful cattle on the yellow sands reclined,
They turn their eyes towards the horizon of the sea,
Their feet towards each other stretched, their hands entwined,
They tell of gentle yearning, frigid misery.

A few, with heart-confiding faith of old, imbued
Amid the darkling grove, where silver streamlets flow,
Unfold to each their loves of tender infanthood,
And carve the verdant stems of the vine-kissed portico.

And others like unto nuns with footsteps slow and grave,
Ascend the hallowed rocks of ancient mystic lore,

Where long ago--St. Anthony, like a surging wave,
The naked purpled breasts of his temptation saw.

And still some more, that 'neath the shimmering masses stroll,
Among the silent chasm of some pagan caves,
To soothe their burning fevers unto thee they call
O Bacchus! who all ancient wounds and sorrow laves.

And others again, whose necks in scapulars delight,
Who hide a whip beneath their garments secretly,
Commingling, in the sombre wood and lonesome night,
The foam of torments and of tears with ecstasy.

O virgins, demons, monsters, and O martyred brood!
Great souls that mock Reality with remorseless sneers,
O saints and satyrs, searchers for infinitude!
At times so full of shouts, at times so full of tears!

You, to whom within your hell my spirit flies,
Poor sisters--yea, I love you as I pity you,
For your unsatiated thirsts and anguished sighs,
And for the vials of love within your hearts so true.

The Death of the Lovers

We will have beds which exhale odours soft,
We will have divans profound as the tomb,
And delicate plants on the ledges aloft,
Which under the bluest of skies for us bloom.

Exhausting our hearts to their last desires,
They both shall be like unto two glowing coals,
Reflecting the twofold light of their fires
Across the twin mirrors of our two souls.

One evening of mystical azure skies,
We'll exchange but one single lightning flash,
Just like a long sob--replete with good byes.

And later an angel shall joyously pass
Through the half-open doors, to replenish and wash
The torches expired, and the tarnished glass.

The Death of the Poor

It is Death that consoles--yea, and causes our lives;
'Tis the goal of this Life--and of Hope the sole ray,
Which like a strong potion enlivens and gives
Us the strength to plod on to the end of the day.

And all through the tempest, the frost and the snows,
'Tis the shimmering light on our black sky-line;
'Tis the famous inn which the guide-book shows,
Whereat one can eat, and sleep, and recline;

'Tis an angel that holds in his magic hands
The sleep, which ecstatic dream commands,
Who remakes up the beds of the naked and poor;

'Tis the fame of the gods, 'tis the granary blest,
'Tis the purse of the poor, and his birth-place of rest,
To the unknown Heavens, 'tis the wide-open door.

Made in the USA
Middletown, DE
21 January 2017